VALARIE,

THANK YOU FOR YOUR INSPIRATION!

The Sorghum Press

Derrick Barksdale

The Sorghum Press

ISBN 978-1-886057-04-3

Manufactured in the United States of America

First Edition

Warren Publishing, Inc.

19722 One Norman Blvd Suite 220-244

Cornelius, North Carolina 28031

www.Warrenpublishing.net

I would like to dedicate this book to my Grandmother Sarah Caldwell.

Every family has a pillar, a statue, a symbol of excellence that stands above the rest. My Grandmother has a powerful Spirit, which illuminates her appreciation of God and his marvelous works. I, as the rest of her family have been blessed to live geographically within her reach and continue to learn from her today. Grandmother, thank you for the inspiration and for being "The Example", which will serve as a valuable tool for generations to come.

CHAPTER I

My Father's Gone

"It's wood until it's sanded." This saying describes how I feel about life. Just as a piece of wood is sanded into a product, our experiences shape us into a product. This process begins the moment we are conceived. Each moment in our life, each experience that we speak of in past tense, has aided in developing us into who we are. Although we watch children reach milestones, we do not often consider how their experiences affect them. People often say, "Children are resilient." We use that expression with confidence, and then, as adults, we accept when people use their past to explain their current condition. The truth is that every experience counts because each one teaches us something. And, although a child may appear to have bounced back from a struggle, there was still a process to surviving it.

The process for me started one day while I was playing on a playground during one of my father's baseball games. All of a sudden, there was a commotion of people, sounds, and moods around me, and, as a child, I didn't understand what was going on. I was confused and troubled, but that was the limit of my reaction to the events unfolding around me because I was too young to recognize the problem, and also I couldn't differentiate between the emotions that others felt and what was actually happening.

During that baseball game, my father fielded a hard-hit ball. Then he went down on one knee. The ball rolled slowly out of his hand onto the field and the game stopped. That's the last memory many have of my father. For me, there would be no more hugs, kisses, or hearing him say, "That's my boy."

Medicine and doctors, I'm sure, were not as advanced as they are today. Doctors diagnosed my father as having muscle spasms, when in actuality my father's heart was failing him.

After the doctors examined my father and dismissed his episode as muscle spasms, he was discharged from the hospital. Before my uncles, aunts, and friends could pick him up to head home, he had a heart attack. My father died there in the hospital, and so started my struggle. I never thought that would happen to me as a little boy. My life had a sudden void, and the chips began stacking against me.

It's funny how simple my thinking was as a young child. In the mortuary I thought, "He is going to get up and walk out of here. We are going to be okay. He is just spending a couple of nights away from us. He will be home soon. All these people are coming because they love us, right?" I did not know they were mourning.

As I struggle to deal with my childhood, I know that I can't let it consume me my entire life. I have vivid images of being in a mortuary, being held up to look at my father's body, and someone touching his face, wondering as a three-year-old child, "Daddy, why don't you wake up? There is no need for you to sleep here anymore. Get out of this bed."

In reality Daddy never got up. In reality my father, that mythical, athletic figure I was a product of, died of cardiac arrest. I really don't know all the details of what actually happened, but it is still painful to think of his death. Pain comes rushing like a roaring river with a flood of tears when I think of the events surrounding my father's death. My connection to him and the image that I have of my father are very vivid in my mind; they are motivational factors for me to succeed. Leaders always use things close to them to continue driving forward. Going through memories and emotions, trying to dig up my past, I'm constantly reminded of how far I have come. I knew that, through the process of writing this book, the tears would flow again and the pain would resurface. But I also knew that I would feel better after I released the tension from some of those memories.

There are memories stamped in my head, but nothing is really connected; there are only pictures, images of what I vaguely remember. My father died two weeks before my fourth birthday. But it's hard to think back before that, even though I can recall some memories from before that time.

People often say that my father was an outstanding athlete. An athlete is something that I longed to become and held on to for many of my young years. Not only did I achieve the status of an athlete, but I became successful at every sport I played. But as a little boy, the pain of not knowing why I was chosen to grow up without my father frightened me. The more I lived, the more the reality set in that my father was gone, that he actually was not coming home. As a young boy, my memory was stamped, not with a playground, not with a baseball, not with people yelling, but with images of my father. My memory is stamped with an image of my father lying helpless.

Why my family? Why would I have to deal with this for the rest of my life? Why would my childhood be pained with the loss of someone so significant? As a three-year-old boy, losing my father was a traumatic experience. Immediately, the stereotypes of a young, black male growing up without a father descended on me.

With the help of family members, my mom, aunts and uncles, I have pieced together good memories of my father that have aided me in getting over the pain of his death. Yes, it is true my father was a superior baseball athlete; he also played football for Sanders Elementary and excelled at it. So the parts that I knew to be great I used to overshadow the parts that are not so great. Being a very young male at the time of my father's death, through most of my childhood I was saddened by his absence. I'm still saddened by the fact that I don't have a father living here on earth. At times in my life I really missed having an example to hold, to look at, and to gaze back at me. Yet, with God's blessings, I have maintained my drive and purpose to excel.

I was a little boy forced into manhood way before what some consider manhood years. I can remember the red telephone left on my father's grave that I retrieved and played with from time to time. In my heart, the red telephone was a way for me to talk to my father. The mementos, the gloves and bats signified that one day I, too, would excel in sports, because he lives through me and I am what he produced. I held onto the bracelets, the trophies and pictures of my father to give me some sense of him. I often looked at the pictures and most times saw my daddy's brothers' images; for this reason, I clamped onto them during my younger years. They gave me a visual of what I was missing. These circumstances forced me to live in a situation that I tried to ignore.

Leaders of tomorrow are sometimes victims of today. As a leader, there are circumstances that you have to adapt to on the fly. Your strength in times of trouble equips others with the hope that they, too, can brave the storm. You're the example of a pure product which will continuously be redefined. Leaders never let voids stand in their way. They fill voids with substance, knowledge, lessons, and, most importantly, love.

Growing up, I watched my mother fix her coffee for the next morning the preceding night before going to bed. Over the years, I learned from this exercise that you always had to prepare for what you knew you wanted the next day or, for that matter, in the future. The filter would go in the top of the coffee pot, three scoops of coffee grains would go in the filter, and then she would fill the pitcher to the 6-cup margin, and finally pour the water in the back of the pot. The next morning, I would smell that coffee brewing, knowing that the product came from my mother's preparation the night before. As leaders, we have to know what to expect by thoroughly preparing. I always knew my mother's final product, her coffee, was going to be hot and ready. Leaders stay hot, they find ways to stay valuable, and they always give the best product that they can provide.

Having intelligent minds, we must be accountable for ourselves and allow our leadership qualities to shine through by our actions. Early in my quest for leadership, I learned to remain humble. A noted speaker once stated that, "Humility is not denying the power or gifting you have, but admitting that the gifting is from God and the power comes through you and not from you."

Being a leader means doing your best work even when people barely know you exist. Take my great-granddaddy Lonnie Caldwell for example, a tall, austere type of man. He very seldom had to say anything, but you knew he was a leader by the way he carried himself. Granddaddy taught me a lesson a long time ago that made me appreciate where I am today. One day he told my cousin Terry and me he would pay us if we helped him do some work around the house, but we had to work hard. So, after a long day assisting him in raking the yard and picking up sticks and leaves, we jumped in his car and Granddaddy said, "I'll pay you when we get to Mrs. Baughman's convenience store." So Terry and I were excited, thinking about all the candy and drinks we were going to buy. We arrived at Mrs. Baughman's store, just bursting about our pay, and Granddaddy reached in his pocket and gave us a quarter apiece.

I was devastated! But I learned from that day forward that, if my granddaddy worked that hard and got paid that kind of money, then I should be mighty thankful of where I am today. I'm thankful for the path that he cleared for me. He struggled through years of civil rights, working in the cotton fields, and going to separate schools because of his ethnic background. His level of humility came from pain, struggles, and love for his family. I often imagine myself in those circumstances, and try to envision what it would be like to be limited in what I could do, yet still have the drive and desire to lead and achieve the unbelievable.

Developing personal relationships with those who have achieved the unachievable gives you wisdom beyond this world. I often think about my grandmother's story of a determined, strong mule that turned an old sturdy press which produced a sweet-tasting product that my taste buds have never let go. The 'Sorghum Press' was strong, solid-standing and erect, braving the elements to get the job done. My grandmother, Sarah Caldwell, comes to mind when I think of the mission of that 'Sorghum Press'. Like the press, my grandmother was not faded by her elements, and, even though she was worn by age, she still stood sturdy and erect as if she had just started her day. Sorghum represents a double crop to some farmers, who use this precious grain not only to feed the cattle, but to make molasses, a complement to any meal. Sorghum is a cereal grass, which, at first glance, resembles corn stalks with large clusters of the sorghum grain on top. It is believed to come originally from Africa, and today, worldwide, it is the third-largest food grain (Cliff Lowe, *Sweet Southern Sorghum*). Sorghum molasses is found throughout the South and is made from the sorghum cane. More impressive than its origin is the process of making sorghum molasses. Through vision and steady effort, farmers of old, and many today, produced something acceptable for use.

In many ways, I think of the 'Sorghum Press' as a metaphor for my family: we have been ground down by circumstances, but ultimately we were molded through the work ethic of a woman who was the epitome of a leader, to produce an end-product which validated her journey through life. My great-granddaddy, Lonnie Caldwell, would set up that mule-driven cane press and Mother (which is what all of her grandchildren and great-grandchildren called my grandmother) used to watch, focused, as the mule, hooked to a long pole, slowly walked around and around turning that cane press. At times Mother would feed the raw cane through the press.

There were three openings in the press: one for cane to go in, one for it to come out, and an opening for the juice of the cane to drain out. Mother paralleled the work of the press by grinding and training the unity that is my family. The sweetness derived from cane after chewed—since it can't be broken, due to its toughness—resembles my family's loving bond, instilled in us by my grandmother.

The sorghum juice was then transferred to an open cooker, cooked and stirred. It was continually checked and manipulated until it reached a level of purity acceptable to the standards of my great-grandmother, Connis Caldwell. Consistency was the ultimate description of my grandmother's work over the years as she steadfastly did the work that was willed to her. She was consistent in her affection and love for each one of her children, grandchildren, and great-grandchildren, making each one of us feel as though we had the number one slot in her heart. There was a knack to this, as the sorghum liquid would reach a point where it was very close to the exact thickness, but still needed some more tending.It is the same with leaders. No one said we, as humans, have to be perfect, but, as leaders, we should consistently strive towards excellence in our lives and with our families. My grandmother's efforts and love went into a family that would reciprocate that feeling and desire to maintain unity. Great leaders take the time to produce greatness. They study their craft, and spend years perfecting it. My grandmother is an expert on my family and the love it takes to maintain unity within it. Store-bought molasses has a generic flavor, but sorghum molasses has a deep, rich flavor that you cannot describe by any words, only by the hard work it takes to produce it.

Like the 'Sorghum Press' on my grandmother's property, consistency makes our lives easier because it creates a routine which we can become accustomed to. Consistency leaves a pattern that we become married to. Consistent leaders are always a homing device for those who are lost in their journey. Great leaders become great because they are consistent at achieving greatness. How many great leaders do you know who have not become an expert at their craft in order to don that title? I would venture to say none, because they had to have the drive to do something and remain consistent at it in order to achieve their goals. Great leaders become consistent with their voice, attitudes, and their work ethic. They promote their leadership through consistency and they remain humble throughout the process.

CHAPTER II

Memories of My Childhood

People interact with you differently when they see a change in your path. I have first cousins who are like brothers and sisters to me. I love them dearly and will do anything for them. Growing up, we had our quarrels, we fell out, but we always knew we would be right back playing after a quarrel. Children can be cruel to each other, but they also have a sense of forgiveness that we lose as we get older. As we get older, that sense of forgiveness hardens; it's no longer there. People feel that there is no need to forgive because we can go home, or wherever we want to go, and not think about that person.

I think back to one Christmas when my cousins and I got dirt bikes. They had Hondas and I had a different kind of motorbike, a more generic brand. We would race, and they would blow me away every time with their Hondas. It would just tear my nerves up as a young boy because I was so competitive and I refused to be unequal to them. Eventually, my motor bike broke down for whatever odd reason, and I had the kind of bike where the throttle was almost like a lawnmower throttle. The wire, attached to a lever, ran to the motor and, the more you lifted the lever, the faster the bike went. Being intuitive and trying to use what I had at the time, I started holding one hand on the wire and one on the handle bar, because I refused to quit and be beaten by my cousins. But, after all of my struggles with that motor bike, the next year my mom bought me a Honda, the biggest, fastest bike on the block. I appreciated that so much because I knew times were hard. I knew I was not able to get one when everyone else got one, but it came.

Sometimes we have to persevere as leaders in order to see our results. Even as a young boy, I didn't feel the need to quit because I had a goal to attain. The reality set in that I wasn't running the race with the same equipment everyone else had, but I refused to quit. Leaders learn to be creative with what they have. When you use what you have, you don't make the mistake of believing that winning depends on external things. "No one is born highly creative," says R. Keith Sawyer, Ph.D, Associate Professor of Education and of Psychology, both in arts and sciences, Washington University. "Psychologists studying creativity have discovered that it is based on cognitive processes we all share. Creativity is not the result of some magic brain region that some people have and others don't." We all have the power to create our success. Regardless of what brand of dirt bike I had, and how I made it go, I had the desire to win. Dr. Martin Luther King Jr. coined it perfectly when he said, "The ultimate measure of a man is not where he stands in moments of comfort and convenience, but where he stands at times of challenge and controversy."

The Grass Incident

I can remember wrestling as a little boy with my cousins, Chris and Terry. Somehow they held me down and put grass in my mouth. My uncle came out and chastised all of us. At the time I felt they had teamed up on me. I started to believe that I was always going to be the victim. I felt that I was always going to be the one who had it the worst, whether it was regarding material possessions, friendship, or love. But when it was all said and done, that day Terry ended up putting grass in his mouth and chewing it in front of me. I assumed that was his way of saying, "I'm sorry."

My cousin Chris had invited me to a sleep over for later that same evening, but I didn't want to go because I felt they had teamed up on me earlier that day. I felt a pain, not because of the grass incident, but because I felt I was alone for some reason. I was talked into coming over, and my uncle could see anger and frustration in my eyes. He knew what had happened with the grass incident earlier, but he saw that I was angry about something more. My uncle Marshall looked me in my eyes and said, "Get it out! Get it out!" I thought, "What do you mean, get it out?" He said, "Slap me!" And thought that this was a setup. "You will beat me if I slap you." He said, "Nobody will whip you. Slap me!" So I reared back and slapped him. And he shouted, "No, slap me harder! I need you to get it out." So that second time I reared back and swung as hard as I could. And he said, "Now, don't you feel better?" And somehow or another I did. That showed me that I would always have family that cared about my feelings. I would always have an outlet and someone to talk to. We benefit from those people we have to talk to.

Leaders can't save the world by themselves. I can't think of any great leaders who won a war by themselves. Leaders have to be conscious of those around them that make their army what it is. Every great leader has great followers. A leader's best assets are his or her following. The relationship a leader has with those followers encourages or hinders positive direction. The day a leader has no following is the day he is no longer a leader.

During my younger years, I came in contact with a lot of people who were inspirational to me. They aided me in building my character and in reinventing who I am. As a race of advanced people, we have to constantly reinvent ourselves to succeed at something different. When we constantly challenge ourselves, we increase our value. We achieve this by forcing ourselves out of our comfort zone and into our growth zone.

Men in my life pushed me into that growth zone. I would look at different men in my life and ask myself, "Is this somebody I want to be like?" I did not identify with any one man as a model, but took attributes from several to help shape who I thought I wanted to be. I have uncles that are still a significant part of my life who helped me grow up, and I don't know if I could ever repay the debt they put on their shoulders.

CHAPTER III

Lessons Learned

To be a leader, one has to offer the world something that changes it. A leader must impact the world, making it different and more exciting. Leaders are unique; they posses an energy people want to be around and learn from. They have their own story that is like no other. As I tell you mine, you will witness the unavoidable hurdles I cleared to become who I am today.

I can't help thinking, over and over, that there are plenty of males from single-parent homes like myself who have gone on to do great things, things far greater than I have. In the educational arena, my highest level of achievement is an MBA degree, which was an accomplishment that I never thought I could achieve. Of course, there are greater stories, because there are people with similar backgrounds that are doctors, lawyers—the list goes on and on—who have changed the world. My struggle has been a psychological one in which I almost destroyed myself believing that only nothingness could come from my situation. Thoughts of not being smart enough, along with many other detrimental visions growing up, slowed my progress, but did not stomp out my fire. My desire to shine, to know more, to be complete, continued to rejuvenate my legs to walk the next mile.

Once I reached certain levels of education, I started wondering if maybe statistics and the world were wrong. Maybe I could get a post-high school education like my counterparts. Maybe I could be on TV one day speaking about how my degrees helped me. But, time and time again, year after year, my surroundings tried to persuade me that I was average, and that I was below any leadership-type position, which I refused to accept. Now I know and trust that I'm a leader. Knowing, believing, and having faith in that is what drives me every day to reach for the unreachable.

The one characteristic that a leader must possess is faith. One must have confidence in oneself that whatever endeavor one has set out to accomplish will be accomplished. Outstanding leaders make decisions based on facts, and apply clearly articulated instructions to accomplish those tasks. Leaders select the right strategy for the right situation, even when the pressure is overwhelming. How many doors have shut in your face and forced you to find another route? Leaders have to force their way towards opportunity, instead of letting opportunity fade away on the horizon while they are caught gazing at it.

Why would people want to read about Derrick Barksdale, a nobody in their eyes? Why would someone want to know my life's story? Well, one reason is that this is not just my story. This is a story about each person who has dealt with the fear of not being good enough for success. This is a story that anyone can relate to because it is proof that we can win battles within ourselves. The truth is: everyone has a personal battle or circumstances that someone else can relate to. One person's battle may be that his family does not have as much as he would like, while another's may be that he has not obtained the level of education that he desires in a world where who you are on paper matters. Simply put, everybody has something to overcome, but the struggle is not so much material, monetary, or anything of that sort. Many of us want these things. However, the struggle is in what it takes to obtain them, that psychological struggle that comes when you believe that your circumstances define your success. When we're constantly told we're not good enough and that we can't succeed, it weighs on our mental focus. We will reach a point, no matter how hard we try, where we can't quite achieve that level that we want to because our psyche will not let us. Our subconscious has a grip on us because it has been trained by our negative environment.

There is a certain level of mental breakdown that begins to happen, even in our early youth. We start believing that we can't succeed. It was not until I started believing I could win the psychological war with myself that my future began to gain clarity. Then it was just a matter of realizing how I needed to adjust my thought processes to set myself in line to win the war. This is an understanding of how the practical, statistics-labeled individual overcomes the psychological war that is going on within. Whether you're White, Black, Japanese, or any ethnicity for that matter, anybody can relate to this inner struggle.

Many of us have experienced events in our family history that have caused us to withdraw from society, that have caused us to think less about ourselves and our situations, and that have caused us to accept the status quo. There is some moment in time that causes us to accept where we are and not dare achieve anything more, out of fear of losing what we already possess. That something makes us think that we should stop while the going is good because we are lucky to have reached the level where we are.

Some of us are content to simply survive, because just surviving is comfortable. We don't have to venture out into the world; we don't have to quit one job and go to the next not knowing whether we will succeed or not. We don't have to go to college; all we have to do is get the basics. Get that high school diploma, go work in the local company and make enough just to pay the bills. It's comfortable, and it's a level of achievement that millions and millions of Americans experience, and it stops right there. The idea of just maintaining is comfortable and fun to some of us, so we end our life-long quest for something better because we are comfortable where we are.

In complacency, we dream about the Mercedes, the BMW, the Escalade, and the big house. We think, "That would be nice, but I'm comfortable and there is no need for me to feel uncomfortable." We never give ourselves the chance to try for those dreams because our satisfaction leads us to believe that this is all they are, dreams. My story is of an individual who refuses to accept being comfortable. I refuse to believe that these are only dreams and define them as desires; therefore, I create goals that incorporate obtaining my desires. Even through some of the struggles and negative habits I still deal with today, I feel confident; I am going to break these habits so they no longer exist in my life nor hinder me from obtaining my success.

We all experience pain. Pain is heavy at times, sometimes so heavy that we put a mask over it. Many of us cover up pain and act as if everything is okay. By doing so, that pain grows and starts oozing outside our mask. So how can we continue to cover up a pain that grows? We can't! The answer is simple. We can't cover up a pain that grows. The only way to corral that pain is to address it head on. We will find that there is pain in life. We must address it head on in order to get over it.

As successful leaders, we have to let go of pain that hinders us from achieving our goals. Letting go of these pains does not mean we have to forget them; it just means we have to accept those pains as a part of our life and begin to use them as building blocks to stepping forward. If we continue to allow our pain to consume us and attempt to deal with it by covering it up, we are allowing it to hinder us. It will continue to bring sorrow, tears, hurtful thoughts, negative vibes, and harsh attitudes towards people that may have aided in creating them. This pain will also cause inhibitions that will destroy future relationships and goals. Writing my story and sharing it is a part of my solution for healing my pain. By telling my story, I am able to defeat my pain and win. I pray others may see a window into their own pain and confront it.

As my story unfolds, my goal is not to be seen as an individual highlighted, but as an opportunity for the reader to identify areas of their lives that need addressing. Reader, make yourself the character, and see yourself overcoming things that you have to deal with on a daily basis. See yourself using your struggles as building blocks to go forward to your destiny.

I have an MBA degree, along with a BA in Art and Design and a diploma in Engineering Graphics. I'm a very creative person, and trying to survive in this world has caused me to turn away from what I enjoy doing, which is art. At one time in my life I thought, "Since I like being creative, drawing, and designing, maybe I'll combine engineering with that and try to make a living doing what I like to do, but on a more technical level." That didn't work; I made a living doing design work, but I also did operational work, inventory, and ran an ink-press machine at the same job. That was a learning experience for me. I learned that having a degree didn't mean I would be working in a field that my degree was tailored for.

I didn't recognize this until many years later, but I found myself conforming to my circumstances, instead of following my heart and doing what really made me happy. That was a difficult puzzle to solve because, as a young adult, I had bills to pay. So I let a situation that I created control my life. I didn't want to be in that situation, but I let a level of comfort control my mindset because I became good at my routine.

My most important life's lesson was this: never become comfortable with a routine that does not bring you ultimate happiness. Whether it is work, school, or hobbies, if you are not happy doing it, do something else.

Although obtaining my MBA was one of the most fulfilling experiences in my life, it was not so much about the degree as it was about achieving that level of success. I really can't say exactly what it was I gained from the degree. There are maybe two or three things I remember from that educational experience that served to enhance my knowledge. But the fulfillment, as sad as it may be, came from saying, "I have an MBA degree." The fulfillment for a long time came from seeing my name on paper with "Masters in Business Administration" beside it. The fulfillment came from people saying, "Oh, you have your Masters!" That meant more to me than the thousands I dished out to pay for the degree, in addition to the stress and the struggles. Two seconds of accolades someone gives can't possibly equate to the two years of pain, struggle, and stress I went through to obtain it. It's amazing what we will do for other people's approval.

I hope my story is able to change thought processes, help individuals who are struggling with something they just can't shake, individuals who have fallen and cannot seem to find a way to get back up. My advice is: get back up! Get back up in front of people, get back up so you can be seen, and understand that nobody can stop you but you. Leaders never let situations control their destiny; rather, they control their situations. How you handle a situation shows your traits as a leader.

CHAPTER IV

Pains of the Past

All of the stories I heard about my father described him as a leader. He was a great athlete, son, brother, and friend. When I saw the guys that he used to play ball with, they would be so excited to see me. I always had the sense that he was loved and admired. Growing up knowing that my father's blood ran through my veins motivated me to have a relentless desire to achieve. I followed only when it was necessary, in order that I might gain the attributes I needed to lead.

Why me? Why was I chosen to be fatherless? Why did God pinpoint me to go through what I went through as a child? Now, as a spiritual man, things are coming clear about why I was chosen. Why *not* me?

I grew up with the mistaken belief that I was not man enough. I didn't have a father, so I coerced myself into believing I was going to be behind, academically and athletically. Some would consider this a mental handicap, but in actuality it was a mental steroid, because I knew I always had to work extra-hard to be better. Things happen for a reason in life. God puts obstacles in our way so we may become stronger.

Sometimes I tried to blanket my childhood memories by mixing truth with fiction. I mixed the reality of what could have been with the reality of what was not. For this reason I felt the need to overcompensate on some things that I thought required my father being there. I have great uncles. These men were willing to step into his place and show me how to be a man. But, somehow, always in the back of my mind, I didn't equate those men with my father.

Those men couldn't ease the pain when I went to sleep at night crying, knowing that my father was not coming back. Those men, as great as they were, couldn't give me the goodnight hug, the holidays, or the Father's Day celebrations. They couldn't give me the graduation days of looking into the stands and seeing both my mother and father being proud together. So, to live and to grow up with this challenge was an everyday fight for me.

Again, there are so many people with similar stories. There are many people reading this book that grew up with other obstacles. It took me twenty-seven years to realize that life is a struggle, but all of life has a purpose. By saying that, I acknowledge that there are good and bad things that happen in our lives. However, it is our decision whether the bad leaves us in turmoil. We have to be able to translate bad circumstances into positive energy and let them become learning experiences. We have to keep increasing our value, hold on to what we know is justified and build on it. We have to do the necessary things that allow us to succeed, regardless of what statistics, people, or our own self-doubts predict. It was not until I forced myself to disagree with others' opinions about me that I could redirect my life and let the strength start showing through the spirituality that was culturing inside me. I had to realize that people could not impede my growth unless I allowed them to do so.

Starting at a young age, I slowly began to realize that my father was never going to be around. The older I got, the more my brain developed, the stronger the pain got, and the more I started to realize that I had something that others did not have. I had something that my first cousins and friends did not have. It was a void that pain, frustration, and confusion were slowly beginning to fill. It was a void that was being attached to my psyche and it was holding steady on me. It was a void that, as I entered my teenage years, I felt growing and hindering my mental growth. No matter how much I covered it up, it grew bigger than any cover I could put on it. I had to find a way to deal with this void instead of simply trying to cover it up.

Is it our circumstances or is it ourselves that cause these voids? Is it things that we can't change that we should dwell on, or is it the things we can change? During my teenage years I asked myself these questions over and over. What is to come? How will I cover up this hurt? How will I be more than a man? Things change, life goes on and unattended pain continues to grow. Pain can be dealt with; however, life can't be stopped. In dealing with pain, we must possess perseverance and faith. Perseverance provides the capacity to continue through the pain, while faith provides the belief that you will overcome this pain. So, where does your faith in the things to come lie?

Successful leaders have a relentless faith. My faith lies in knowing there is an especially tailored plan created just for me. Faith helped me through some of my more turbulent times. I had an inner calling, and even though I ignored it most of my young adult life, I still recognized it in my subconscious. Sometimes I told fairy-tale stories about myself to others in order to make myself feel better about who I was. As wrong and as strange as it sounds, most of those stories, although not completely true, trained my subconscious to believe in the person I wanted to be.

As true leaders, we must think ourselves into victory. Will anyone follow us if we don't follow our own thought processes? Will anyone believe in us if we don't believe in ourselves? Will we be able to assemble minds to generate profitable beliefs, if our own minds do not? Simple questions, but they all have complicated answers. Transferring our faith to others will allow us to collectively move mountains in any situation.

Robert Greenleaf states, "Leaders must have more of an armor of confidence in facing the unknown, more than those who accept their leadership. This is partly anticipation and preparation, but it is also a very firm belief that in the stress of real life situations one can compose oneself in a way that permits the creative process to operate." Most of us are at our best when we are put under time constraints, when stress enters the picture. Sometimes we run faster when something is after us. In my life I had to run fast often; as a result, I developed a quest for speed. My hunger to do what I thought I couldn't do in life has aided me in my development. When one is not allowed to construct a thought, one is forced to use stored information. This makes one depend on a past reservoir of knowledge. This feat can be amazing to some individuals who don't believe in their conscious thought process. The old verb "can't" always enters the picture, because we inherit that belief by not facing the unknown. Until you fail at something, you really can't learn how to succeed at it. If there was not a process to our achievement, we would all have riches beyond our imagination, because we would instantly desire things that make our natural world easy to exist in, and then there would be no such thing as success.

What should we choose to nurture our motivation? Should it be what we know can be changed, or should we continue to mull over the things we can't change? As we grow older, the majority of us get smarter. True growth requires the desire to grow and mature. My leadership qualities continue to grow because I long for the ability to lead and to be the father I never had in my life. I long for the abilities that they said I wouldn't have because of my bloodline. Yes, I'm a Barksdale, and, as I redevelop myself, I also redevelop the pain that I went through and use it to build my life.

As a child, I knew my daddy was gone and Momma was hurt and frustrated. In the blink of an eye, there was an obstacle-course called life that I had to stumble through without a father. How could I do this? How could I deal with this pain that people said would get easier, but only grew along with me?

The older I got, the more I tried to hold onto items of my father's that created a fading hope. I only had stories that were countered by my reality. What should I tell my mother when she cried at night wondering how we were going to make it? What should I tell Momma when I knew she was stressed and frustrated, worrying that things might not be alright, but faithfully praying that they would?

As a young child, I was teary-eyed most of the time and didn't even know why. But as I got older, the pain became greater and the mask that covered my fears became more creative. There is a hint of that pain that I deal with constantly. There is always an ongoing struggle to overcome the pain and transform it into motivation instead of allowing it to tear me down. Instead of tearing me down, my fears become convictions. I will ensure that my family is taken care of and that my son has a father that he can respect all his days. So I go forward, knowing that the Lord sees in me something that is beyond greatness, something that he will inevitably cultivate to use and mold the minds of millions.

But as a little boy no one saw that. They saw a hard-headed and frustrated individual. They saw an individual who probably would not amount to anything, who would probably end up in jail, much like those around him. They saw an individual who caught a bad lick in life, an individual who they wished in their minds would fail because his failure would prove what they believed about their own state. But he continued to push forward, thus beginning the life of that old, rusty, termite-infested block of wood. The abstract visualization of what could be.

As leaders, we have to visualize solutions to problems and implement them. Leaders are sound thinkers. They merge their subconscious thoughts with conscious decisions. I learned growing up that no one would believe in my subconscious visions, but they would follow my conscious actions. So my ability to lead was not as complicated as I thought. It was merely acting on what I thought in my subconscious mind to be great. Of course, this was not as easy as it sounds.

I didn't know how it was going to get easier. My surroundings constantly reminded me that it was going to get harder before it got easier. The pain was going to grow before it ceased, but somehow, throughout my life, I believed that there would be an end to it. As I stated earlier, pain has to be transformed into motivation. We have to make the decision to use our pain to develop negative or positive energy. As negative energy it swells in us and produces failure. As positive energy it motivates change and provides avenues to overcome the circumstances that caused the pain. At some point I had to start focusing on the goal of the pain being over. I focused on the goal that one day all my pain and sorrow would not be in vain. It is the process that molds our lives. John Higman, author of *Ethics Leadership in America*, explains, "At best it is a difficult matter to identify a group's leadership. We are seldom certain what we are looking for. As for the Afro-American, much of the historical leadership is lost to us because we have not been much interested in the process by which individuals such as Harriet Tubman or the numberless anonymous black men and women who helped to organize the underground railroad or to disrupt the administration of the antebellum fugitive slave laws were identified and accepted by others as leaders. We have focused on the hero rather than the process." So many times we focus on the person before our eyes instead of the process that built that person to be who he or she is.

Leaders see the end result before it comes to fruition. They connect all the pieces to the puzzle without touching one piece. Being sound leaders, we have to complete the final product before anyone else has a clue what it will look like. Doing so requires a sound process, step-by-step procedures. We must know where we are stepping in the dark by continuing to focus on the light. We have to gain confidence in our decisions by giving trustworthy directions toward an end goal that nobody sees but ourselves. True leaders meet obstacles and consume the trouble before others around them get a chance to analyze what the trouble is.

CHAPTER V

How I Put What I Learned to Use

During my 7th grade year, I encountered yet another hurdle in my life, which would prove to be life-changing. For the first time in my life, I was told by the administration at my school that I was not smart enough to remain in above-standard classes. I was told that I would be placed in a remedial math class because my standardized test scores indicated that I could not do the work of an average student my age. This hurt, and it set me back: I was being placed in a class with kids whom I was guilty of picking on because they were deemed slow or below average. Now I was sitting in a class with these same students, wondering how and why this happened to me!

So, as my 7th grade year progressed, my insecurities grew, and, even at the young age of twelve or thirteen, I was humbled by being in this remedial math class. My mother was told at parent-teacher conference meetings that my performance indicated I did not need to be in this remedial class. However, this experience challenged my self-esteem and required me to mature in the ways I viewed other people. I excelled in this class. The work was easy for me, and I made straight A's. My teacher, Mrs. Adam, used me to help other students in that class who needed help. My desire that year was that we would all succeed in order to change the stereotypes that were placed on students in remedial classes. I now knew, firsthand, the same pain, frustration, and embarrassment that others had encountered in these classes, because I was a part of that experience. I became identified by my group instead of my individuality.

I was able to talk to and develop friendships with people that I, at one time, thought I was better than and therefore didn't associate with. I was able to have conversations with students whom I deemed "not like me". While developing those relationships, I realized that most of these new friends had been dealing their entire academic careers with the pain and frustration that I was first experiencing that year. It became clear that year that there were people out there in greater pain than me and in bondage to a system they couldn't defeat. I believe, without a doubt, that there are millions of students out there who can't defeat the system because the system has them pegged, based on the system's methods instead of each individual student's learning progression. I learned several things in that class, but the one thing that stood out above the rest is that no one is above anyone else when it comes to personal value.

James Burns states, "The powerful influence of peer groups in molding social attitudes is as evident to the casual observer as it is in the findings of numberless studies. The price of group membership is conformity to prevailing norms, whether in urban high schools or in the Soviet Union or in an elite college like Bennington, where a classic study demonstrated the acceptance by prestigious peer groups required allegiance to liberal norms." Leaders must constantly ask themselves, "Whom do I influence?" Until leaders know the type of people they are attracting, they can't appropriately gauge their success. If the Pied Piper blew his flute and attracted dogs instead of mice, surely he would have rethought his playing process. You attract what you may or may not want to attract; for this reason, we constantly have to reassess ourselves and our direction.

8th Grade

I went on to the 8th grade and was placed into above-standard classes, though the label of not being smart enough followed me for a while. I had to make the decision either to carry this label or to break the stereotype. Surely there was only one answer for me, knowing that it would be a difficult fight. But even then, I had to gain control of my path.

I did fine in the 8th grade and it was time to go to high school. As a part of the process to enter the 9th grade, I had to develop a schedule of classes I thought I should take. The process was to obtain a schedule sheet and have your teachers suggest a course plan that stated which section of classes you needed to take, A, B or C. A lot of parents and students never challenged the teacher's decision because they considered the teachers to be professionals who should know best. Well, knowing that I didn't want to go through the pain that I went through in junior high, I kind of smudged my class schedule. Yes, I got recommendations on what I should take, but I knew in my heart I was smarter than what I was being given credit for.

So, I scheduled classes a level higher than the administration advised me to. Boy, was I scared! I didn't want to flunk out of school and I knew that I had gone against what was advised for me. Due to the nonchalant attitudes of the administration at the time, no one followed through on my changes, so I was able to go on to high school and study on an academic level that would prepare me for college. That was the single most valuable decision I made in my life; I would not be where I am today if it were not for that decision. Sometimes leaders make decisions even when no one else believes in them.

While preparing for high school academics, I also had to prepare for high school sports. I spent the summer before my 9th grade year lifting weights and taking amino acids and protein. I had to hide my supplements because, in that era, my mother thought anything I took besides a Bayer aspirin was an illegal drug! So, in order to keep peace in my home, I privately nurtured my own physical development. But I reinvented myself so that, when I stepped onto the field, I would not be an average player.

From grade school through my high school years, I played sports: baseball, basketball, football, and track. During my younger years, I excelled at baseball more than at any other sport. Every year I played, I was selected to go to the All-Stars, where the best players were chosen from each team at the end of the season to represent the county. I played sports because it kept my mind distracted from a lot of things I would have to deal with if I were not playing.

I was an average football player in junior high. Many people were used to me being average and accepted that. But I had a revelation during the summer of my 8th grade year. I thought to myself, nobody knows that I'm an average player when I get to high school. So I'm going to reinvent myself. I started lifting weights, running, and taking protein, all the things that an athlete would do normally to increase his performance.

When I got to high school, the competition was a lot fiercer than it had been in junior high. The guys were bigger, stronger, and faster than what I was accustomed to. Of course I was nervous, but I found out that, due to my preparation, I was one of the stronger and faster athletes. My mindset changed because I was no longer viewed as average. I could compete on a level equal to or higher than most of the guys around me. Day after day my mindset strengthened because I had prepared myself to exceed the average, and that's exactly what took place. My 10th grade year I was moved up to play varsity during the playoffs.

Now, what does this all mean? Let me explain. Leaders put themselves in a position to exceed the normal. They push themselves past the low expectations that they may have been labeled with or even set themselves. By exceeding the average, my mindset would not let me go back to playing second- or third-string football. I only wanted to play first-string football because playing behind someone was not an option for me. Now, of course, if coach had said, "Barksdale, you are third-string tonight", then I would have been forced to be third-string, but my mindset would not allow me to believe that I was only good enough to play third-string.

Preparing for something greater allows us to overlook the small setbacks that may frustrate us. God has allowed me to prepare for something greater. Many of us, whether we know it or not, have already exceeded the average. Many good candidates were turned down for the very position we are sitting in now. See, in our daily walk we are placed in situations or constraints that we should know we are greater than. If we are making ten dollars an hour and we know we're worth twenty, then why aren't we doing the things required to equip ourselves with the skills to get twenty dollars an hour? We have to move. Our mindset must not be trained to stand still. We have to keep going regardless of the situation. Do not be overwhelmed by limitations. We must work to enhance our abilities and overcome these obstacles.

I lost my grandmother, my father's mother, during my high school years. She was my connection to my dad's side of the family. My grandmother was the stronghold for that side of the family. I loved my grandmother dearly and I know I should have shown it more while she was living. I hoped that she would be around when I graduated high school and college, so that I could show her that she was correct about me, that I had become the person she thought I would. I wanted her to know that I went on to do what others said I couldn't do. For her love and support I am thankful.

The stress we go through in losing loved ones leaves us unprepared. And every time we see a loved one lying in a casket, it multiplies our feelings for each person we have lost before. So, during my youth, it was hard for me to go to funerals. And even as an adult, I am only now embracing the fact that death is okay. The fact is, the more I love God and Jesus Christ, the more my motivation to see my loved ones again grows. My confidence is strengthened that we will be one again.

The Master in You!!

We know why we let ourselves lose: we constantly depend on other people to give us the satisfaction of success. We let others measure whether or not we are successful. How can we improve ourselves if we're not motivated to do so? I used to sit and sulk because of the cards I was dealt growing up: how I didn't have a father; how I missed the normal family condition and had no brothers or sisters to interact with. I wondered, since I had been dealt all of these bad cards, when were some good cards coming? Day after day I would beat myself up because of my circumstances, until I figured out that the only one keeping me from accomplishing what I wanted to accomplish was myself!

CHAPTER VI

The Reinvention

How do we reinvent ourselves?

I had several opportunities in my life to reinvent myself. Going into my 12th grade year, I was an average student. In my mind, I still felt I placed behind a lot of my classmates because of standardized tests. I graduated with what I would deem an average student's learning, even though I was an honor-roll student and received an academic letter my senior year. Yet, in academic ranking, I fell in the middle of my class. To this day I still think the system tagged me. I had restraints on me that, no matter what kind of grades I had, I couldn't break. I still had the reputation for being a smart student by my peers, which probably counted for more than how the school viewed me. I don't even remember if I used guidance counselors at all when applying for colleges.

I was accepted into Winthrop University during my senior year, which was kind of close to home. I followed family tradition instead of going two or three states away, because I still had family and emotional ties restraining me. About five of my cousins had attended Winthrop before me.

College

My college years were some of the most troubled times of my life. I had a tight-knit group of friends that had my back in a lot of instances. But, at the same time, I never knew who my friends were. I fell into a situation where they were needed. Some people proclaim to be a friend just to take part in the image-hype that surrounds you, because they think association with you will make them more popular. In actuality, I developed an image that took a long time to erase, and to this day I'm still haunted by some of the actions and decisions I made during college. I think back and wonder to myself, "Would I want that for my son? Would I want him doing some of the things I did?" The answer is, absolutely not, which is why I find myself trying to be an example of what I want him to be. I just hope that it does not take him as long as it took me to find out who he really is.

During those years I met many people from different walks of life. But there were very few I met who really cared about my future. There were people who cared about me, but no one really cared about my future. I don't know if *I* cared about my future. Even after graduating college with a BA in Arts and Design, it really didn't mean anything to me. Most people would describe that experience as an exciting accomplishment, but for me it was more something to get out of the way so that I wouldn't have to be bothered by a schedule, or a professor telling me I had to turn something in at a certain time anymore. I paid my university thousands of dollars for housing, education, and meals for four years. I found it all a waste. The story that was painted for me my whole life was: go to college, graduate, and get a good job. In actuality that's not really how it works, because I followed that plan. I was expecting to wear a button-up shirt and a pair of slacks to work every day.

Well, I got to wear a button-up all right, but I was buttoning up my overall worksuit with my name patched on it. Most people today call it a uniform. And I needed my uniform because I ran an ink press.

"Mr. Degree, Mr. Smart Man, you are running an ink press making eight dollars an hour. Is that what you struggled through four years of college to achieve?" There were people working in warehouses making more money than I was, and they hadn't paid a university thousands of dollars to do it. "Where is your worth with this expensive education? What tags you as knowing more with a college degree?" My degree didn't mean anything when it came to my bank account.

The realization set in fast that it wasn't just obtaining a piece of paper proclaiming this degree or that degree, but it was applying my experiences that would lead me to succeed, the application that should have been happening all through college, but nobody told me about. We go to college and get in a fraternity, sorority, or organization, work to become an athlete, or whatever the case may be, and we tend to cover up the value of self. There is so much hype around us that we become caricatures instead of individuals, and we believe our caricature has some value. We look at how much people want to be a part of our clique and we believe we are important.

In actuality, what other people want adds no value to who we are as individuals. It is equivalent to buying a brand-new Mercedes, putting 22-inch chrome wheels on it and televisions in the headrests, expecting the value of it to increase. Yes, it looks good right now, but undoubtedly that car becomes a depreciating asset. So where is our value? How do we save ourselves from allowing others to measure our worth?

Embrace change in your mindset. Be humble in your brilliant approach to change. Just because our environment or the people around us say that we're not good enough, don't believe them. They want us to remain in place because we will then prove their statements correct. The most brilliant man who walked the earth said it perfectly; "Get thee behind me Satan" (Matthew 16:3, King James Version). If we allow people to keep our minds imprisoned, they will always hold the keys to our freedom. Let me say this again: if we allow someone to keep our mind imprisoned, then that someone will always hold the keys to our freedom. I don't know about you, but I don't want to fulfill someone else's prophecy telling me and my family that I'm not going to be successful just because I constantly listened to, took in, and believed all of their insults. I can't imagine someone telling me, "You fail because I say you fail." Believe me, that is another book on how many times I was told I would fail and not amount to anything. Be the master of your mindset, control your environment, and know you're blessed.

Dr. Dennis Kimbro once stated, "Like physical effort, thought control is entirely a matter of intelligent practice. You must use your courage or it will desert you. You must use your determination or it will leave you. You must use your power of decision or soon you will find that you have none." As leaders, we have to practice our inherited desire to lead. The most important feature we possess is our mind, and most of us never exercise it. Dr. Kimbro speaks of losing what we don't use. This is not a "store up for the winter" life we are living; we must continue to exercise our minds to endure the journey of life.

Every mental stimulus our minds entertain triggers a physical response to it. Simply put, our bodies act according to what our minds instruct them to do. Therefore, our bodies must be in complete unison from head to toe, because, regardless of how many parts it has, they are all still considered one. Our minds can make our bodies feel as if we have no energy to perform our day-to-day activities. Yet we know that we have performed these activities many times in the past with the same, if not more, energy. Energy is generated by the mind and then released through the body. It cannot be destroyed, but it can be released. In an effort to control our energy, we must have a goal in mind to release it towards. If not, that energy will be controlled by someone else.Without guidance, that energy could be headed toward destruction, failure, or some involuntary action created by our own mismanagement. Our subconscious has to be in complete obedience to our conscious directions.

Many of the ideas planted in our minds are from other people and our own circumstances. Regardless of the path, we will always have the opportunity to act on those ideas. Leaders constantly think of success as an ultimate goal. A plan is made and then focused upon until success is reached. For instance, many Olympic sprinters have one thing in mind when competing: to cross the finish line first. All of the endorsements, commercials, and paychecks for finishing do not matter at the moment they cross the finish line. What matters is that they came in first!

Everyone in this world has a goal in life. Many don't reach their goal because they lack the ability to tap into their subconscious mind. It's there, go get it, bring it to the forefront, and act on it with the conscious mind.

CHAPTER VII

The Real World

In my mind, I found myself limited in what I could do. I found myself around people who had limited themselves. I trained my subconscious to believe that not applying myself and not increasing my value was okay, because I had created a self-limiting atmosphere in which people accepted those attitudes. As successful people, we have to break boundaries and stop creating limitations for ourselves. Many young adults find themselves in this state. They have an okay job and believe it's okay to stay complacent. They think, "I want the dream job, but what I have is okay for right now." Before long, five to ten years have passed. and it's still okay.

So what do we do to increase our value? First, we put ourselves in an environment where pressure is constantly applied. We need pressure constantly in our paths, which forces us to perform. And if you don't perform, there are consequences to pay. We must put ourselves in situations where people depend upon our decisions.

Leaders constantly put themselves in situations that force them to achieve. Leaders only pass through neutral, they never stay in it. They maintain the mentality that only the strong will survive. If they don't work on being great, they will never become great. If they don't work on being a great speaker, they will never become a great speaker. If they don't work on leading, they will never become a leader. They have to put themselves in situations where they must grow or get run over. They will survive and flourish. Leaders surround themselves with people who want them to survive and flourish.

Mr. Clark

A man came into my life during my early twenties who was very inspirational in my development as a leader. This man contributed much to my mental success. Mr. Clark forced me to survive and flourish.

After running an ink press right out of college with a degree, I came across Mr. Clark and his wife, Mrs. Clark. I grew very close to them over the years. While working for this man, my responsibilities slowly began to grow. In all of my academic career, I never met anyone as smart as Mr. Clark. I started out with small jobs in his company; but slowly I began to push myself to take on more. Eventually I became operational manager of Mr. Clark's company. Becoming operational manager forced me to learn every function of the company. It forced me to learn every machine, participate in design work, and learn accounting, which was Mrs. Clark's responsibility. Mrs. Clark was excellent with numbers. It was a building-block effect; I couldn't just become thorough in one area. They forced me to know the company inside and out. My experience with them will aid me in running my own company one day. I learned the ins and outs, pains, struggles, and the joys that come with running a company.

Mr. Clark was incredibly knowledgeable. He could talk about people, events in history, and things that made me look at him in awe. I often asked myself, "How does he know so much? Why isn't he traveling the world with all of that knowledge? Who has all of this knowledge and retains it? How can he know so much about this world, this country, business, computers, money, and labels?" I still struggle with that to this day. It isn't enough to simply say he was smart. He could have successfully done several different things with his life. This man taught me things about spirituality, financial deficits, investments, the position the world was in, and who really controlled the money markets of the world. Those are the things I carry with me from my experiences with Mr.and Mrs. Clark.

Business was not all they taught me. It was the things that were not work related that I benefited from the most, things I learned outside the job. As our relationship grew, I felt like a part of their family. I felt I could go to their home anytime I needed to. I could call anytime I wanted to talk. What a wonderful feeling, to have someone around that could give such profound advice. Sometimes I was not ready for the direction that was given to me. Mr. Clark refused to let me be comfortable and he refused to let me be complacent. Mr. Clark was not only a mentor to me but also a great leader in my eyes. He had a passion for teaching and inspired me to develop into a leader. Mr. and Mrs. Clark made me push the envelope. They not only put me in a position to succeed, but allowed me to fail, and I'll never forget them for that.

The tragedy of confusing leadership with power will prevent some of us from becoming leaders. Running a company and becoming the next senior leader is no good if your team does not believe in what you're doing. Never separate yourself from those on whom you depend. A great leader has served first. There is no greater experience than to humble ourselves to someone who has traveled the journey before. Great leaders are willing to shout out the navigational instructions so we don't fall in the holes they have already encountered.

We must recognize which people around us care and we should gravitate toward them. We cannot stay still and make the world come to us. We have to move ourselves into avenues that can offer change and growth. Leaders have the ability to find open paths. They possess freedom through success. Not until they reach their goals do they feel a complete level of satisfaction and accomplishment. Obstacles are temporary; victory is a permanent achievement.

As I sit here, I am confident that God has moved me to a place I can accept. He has moved me to a place in which I can embrace the person I have become. I now live cautiously, because I recognize that I'm viewed as an example. I know somebody is ready to scrutinize the way I used to live and use that to justify that I do not deserve the joy I have now. I realize I have the ability to lead, and the ability to get people to follow me, regardless of what the scenario or the situation is.

Growing up, I saw that I influenced others. However, I didn't realize the consequences I would face, as would those who followed me, until I understood the responsibility behind my leadership. Some of the things that I did I'm not particularly proud of, but somehow I was strong enough to get through a lot of the bad situations. On the other hand, some of those who followed me didn't quite make it. I'm now learning that what I say around my friends, family, and peers can be detrimental. I accept that people will follow me and that, due to that influence, I can lead others down the wrong path or towards life's endless possibilities.

CHAPTER VIII

The Graduate

Get your MBA!!! Join that elite, diverse group of individuals who push change in the way our world operates. Become empowered to talk intelligently on the state of the global economy; study to develop an international presence in marketing, management and corporate strategy. Doesn't this sound good? Doesn't it give us hope for tomorrow? Just go back to school and become the prized individual that so many Fortune 500 companies fight over. Isn't that what we have been taught? Isn't it easy to achieve an MBA? Job offers are going to start flowing our way, right? Right?!

My answer is no, No, NO! We seek things that sound empowering, but rarely do we ever empower ourselves with the necessary attributes to be successful. Everything I said previously about the MBA degree was embedded in my consciousness. Go back to school and land a big job in two years. In reality, I gained another degree that I somehow had to make work for me. No big jobs waiting, no salary increase, and no promotions. Nothing changed after I got my degree. I don't want to discredit my MBA, but millions of people will go back to get a graduate degree just for the satisfaction of knowing they can. For me, to get my MBA was to say to the world, "I am a professional, so look at me with respect."

Shortly after graduating, I figured out that it was not necessarily the degree that aided me in advancement, but the application of the principles I learned while obtaining the degree. I had the knowledge, but did I have the will power to create success for myself? Did I know what to do with the powerful education I had in order to create opportunities for myself and others?

What did I apply? That's the catch. There are things I learned in graduate school that were applicable to a certain area or interest that would open avenues for me to advance. Whether I took those roads or not was the key to the puzzle. I certainly didn't at first. I knew that an MBA degree didn't coincide with technology the way I wanted it to, but eventually my MBA degree would give me an edge and get me ahead in my professional career. It's almost like I stored up for the winter with my credentials to say, "I'm approved."

How did this happen? What was the process that took place to push me over the hump? First understand, I was an average student. I scored in the average range on standardized tests, and I was an average college student, but I found a crack in all of this to survive. I had an exceptional imagination which put me in a lot of situations where I had to perform in order not to fall. I imagined one day I would have an MBA degree, I would work for a large corporation, and I would eventually motivate thousands through my speaking. No matter what my circumstances were at the time, I always imagined I would be great. We have to ask ourselves, why not? Constantly I asked myself *why not?* Who is keeping me from inspiring others with my experiences? Who is keeping me from becoming an MBA graduate? Who is keeping me from getting my PhD? Who is keeping me from gaining anything I choose in this wonderful land of opportunity? The pointer always came back to me. I had to quit thinking like the average thinker and start thinking like the greatest leaders that ever walked this earth.

I started telling myself, "If you want to go back to grad school, then do it! If you want to be more than average, you have to stop being complacent!" Once I got into grad school, I was forced to be more than average, which is consistent with most business schools today. There is a level above average which you must maintain to get the degree. I had to continue defeating the fear that I was academically average.

I had to push the envelope. Was I scared? Yes! Was I nervous? Yes! Did I think I would fail at some point? Yes! Actually, I took one class two or three times and I thought that class would get me kicked out of grad school. But I refused to imagine myself without this degree. I found myself fighting a battle that I created because I had put myself in an environment that wouldn't let me be average. These are the decisions we face. We have to put ourselves in a mindset that refuses to let us accept mediocrity. We must rise above that level, and until we reach that level, we will always find ourselves being passed by someone else, because they refuse to maintain the status quo. Our path to leadership should, at some point, combine our enthusiasm with our ability to motivate.

I graduated with an MBA degree and worked at a help desk, doing work that did not require a master's level degree to do. A short time after receiving my degree, I was overlooked for certain positions and remained constant in my mindset for over a year. I fell into a depreciating state with a post-graduate degree in my hand. I played the story line in my mind, over and over again. Go to college and obtain an undergraduate degree, go back to school, get the MBA degree, and it will make a difference. I followed all the steps to a tee. I achieved the degrees just as the book of "supposed to be" stated I should.

The truth of the matter was that, although this degree had prestige, it meant less without experience. We must ensure that we are more than an educated asset who provides no immediate value to a company.

What happened next? The MBA holder receives opportunities while the two- or four-year degree student gets looked over because the MBA person holds the bigger title. Ask yourself, if you had an MBA graduate seeking one of your positions and a two-year technical student seeking the same position, to whom would you give the opportunity? I think many of us know the answer; the world is a place of titles and popular names. Value is often hidden by these things. In many cases we would hire the loud, frustrated, over-certified individual, rather than the hard-working, honest, focused on doing a great job individual, because of a title.

Even the system for which this supposedly valuable education is being taught has failed us as a society. We have the academic PhD professors teaching the social disciplines, applying a scholarly coat to the information being received. There is very little real-world experience being taught in our academic environments. We need to seek out those individuals who have walked the walk we are about to set out upon. In addition to the classroom knowledge, we need to allow someone to enhance our education with their experiences. Great leaders provide real-world experiences because they have lived it, failed at it, tried again, and succeeded at it. The lessons they can teach will provide insight about their journey to being great. They will teach that true leaders cannot conform to ideas of the masses. However, they took some time to follow, in order to obtain the necessary skills to lead.

We follow the majority more than we invest in leadership. Following someone should be a stair-step to our ultimate goal, which is to become a leader. We must listen to learn. What we hear has a bearing on how we act. Whether good or bad, we have some reaction to it. But what do we do once we have this knowledge? We exercise that knowledge by applying it. If we conform our whole life to following, we will miss the ship of leadership. Notice that I describe leadership as a ship, because it's bigger than life, strong, sturdy, and millions of people want to brave the stormy sea, but only on this ship. Simply put, leaders are a safe haven for those who always want to follow. They feel protected, they don't worry about making the big decisions, and they want to remain in their comfort zones. Leaders must break out of this way of thinking before it consumes us. Great leaders visualize, but most importantly, they lead with specific direction. For instance, think back your childhood when somebody screamed loudly and started running. What did we have the tendency to do? We would take off running too, without knowing what we were running from. Sadly, this parallels too many of our unquenchable quests in life. We follow aimlessly without knowing our direction. We do what the masses do because, if enough people are doing it, it must be right.

In working through my corporate career, some stated at times, "You are crazy for working for what you are getting paid. You have an MBA; you should be at least making this amount. If I were you, I would go do contract work; everyone does it and comes back to earn what they should salary-wise." We all have unique circumstances which mold us into the people we are. If how much I made in salary described my value, then I would have been in a mental institute a long time ago. No, my salary did not make me any more valuable than if I had a million dollars. My value comes from my personal growth, lessons learned from my struggle to achieve and, last but not least, my ability to love and be loved by those around me.

Consider your value as a lifetime investment that continues to gain interest. Never settle for simple edification. Increase your value to the world by increasing who you think you are. Here are a few steps to follow when doing so:

1. Set yourself at a higher price rather than at a bargain-basement price. For some odd reason, people associate the higher price as being better. This example

can be seen in almost everything around us. Look at the expensive cars in comparison to the economy-style vehicles. Luxury, price, name—all of these things weigh in your decision to purchase, and usually you buy for those things rather than purchasing for reliability, miles per gallon, etc.

2. Offer to provide your service for free. Many will have a problem with this one, but how many CEOs get top-notch candidates for free these days? You are viewed as being confident in who you are; therefore, the decision to pay you what you are worth will come sooner than expected.

3. Highlight your positive points. Don't waste time with all of the murky buildup. Clearly state what you offer and why, up front! When salesmen are trying to sell a product, they don't waste time with the boring details; rather, they highlight the attractive ones.

4. Believe in yourself by proving, beyond a shadow of a doubt, who you are. If you don't believe in you, They won't believe in you. While playing sports in junior high, I really didn't believe that I was a good athlete. Once I knew I had a chance to start over in high school, I believed I was a superb athlete and performed on that level.

5. Get signoff by someone who has been there. It's called references, but don't just use them on resumes, use them anytime. When people know you have been influenced and trained by the best, you become more attractive to them.

And, combined with all of these items stated above, have an imagination. I gained a degree without creatively constructing a path to upward mobility. This proved damaging to my drive for a short time, until I slapped myself out of this state.

CHAPTER IX

The Upward Climb

What changed in the equation that made the world recognize Derrick Barksdale? What changed was twofold: my mindset and my thought process. I took ownership of my own faults and stopped pointing the finger at others. My situation became what I made it. As great leaders, we have to remind ourselves that our situations are the way they are because we made them that way.

What did I do to change my situation? I began calling and emailing people in my professional environment for advice. While working at the help desk, I talked to a lot of people, from the bottom to the top of the company. In talking to these people, my service never changed, regardless of who called in. So I maintained a superior work ethic. I strived to serve everyone as if he or she were the CEO of the company.

That proved to help me, because one day I took a call from a gentleman who didn't quite know how to use the technology he had. The average call would take me about five to ten minutes; this particular call took two hours. As I helped this individual, he began to ask questions and find things out about me. The more I told him, the more he became concerned and involved with who I was, and why I was doing what I was doing and not moving up in the corporation. During the call, he invited me downtown to meet him, and from there he started to mentor me on some of the things I needed to do. The more he advised me, the more he made me realize that I needed to do more than what I was doing if I wanted to move. He made me understand that my mind was too valuable for me to remain still. This gentleman made me look at myself and say, "If one door closes, you have to look for another door." I started looking for those doors and the more I searched, the more opportunity came my way.

One day my manager came to me and told me that there was a diversity training class being offered, which at the time was a corporate initiative. She asked if I wanted to go. My answer at the time was, no. She replied, "There are senior vice presidents attending this class. You need to attend." Then I asked, "Will there be others in this class like me?" Of course, the whole point of diversity training for the workplace meant that there probably *wouldn't* be others like me, but it so happened that the head of my line of business was in this same diversity training class, although he didn't know me—nor did I know him. It's strange how God puts people in our paths. During our week-long training, this top executive got to know Derrick. He got to know Derrick's past, he got to know Derrick's beginnings, and Derrick's struggles. Towards the end of the week, this executive walked up to me and asked, "Why are you doing what you are doing with the education you have? You have a lot to offer this company." And I answered, "I've tried! I've posted for jobs; I've posted for areas where I could contribute and grow, but I've been told over and over, 'we have found someone more suitable for this position'." It's sad, because there were a thousand more people just like me, but were unable to be seen or heard.

On that day I finally started to think, maybe it's not the all-important sounding resume; maybe it's diversifying your portfolio. And I'm not talking about stocks; I'm talking about the people you associate yourself with day-in and day-out. Why not reach out and meet somebody you don't know? Why not have a conversation with a stranger and find out if you have something in common?

This individual was puzzled by my position. We developed a relationship after that; more than that, we developed a friendship that would prove to be very valuable to my career, not because this person had a powerful position with the company, but because he had experience and valuable insight that helped me develop. He gave me direction and inspiration. He had traveled the bomb-infested path and was willing to share his map with me on how to navigate through.

Leaders take time to become aware of their surroundings. They know who is working for them and who they are working for. Leaders have to know the terrain in order to navigate strategically over it. People are around us because they want to be. Don't overlook those people who want to be around you, while focusing on those who could care less about your success.

As time passed and more opportunities popped up, I had the chance to enter an information technology associate program. This program was tailored to bring in the brightest students from across the country and train them for leadership positions. I was one of sixteen applicants chosen to come through this program. There were decisions to be made after being accepted. Would I accept the position? How would I feel being a graduate student coming through this program, having worked at the same company for three years? What kind of image would this send to other individuals coming down the same path I had? Would this aid me in moving up in this company?

I didn't really know how this associate program would benefit me at first, but one thing I did know was that it presented change. It pushed me out of my complacency with the status quo. Coming through this program, I met young, bright students from all over the world, as well as senior vice presidents, and I began to rub elbows with people I normally would not have had the chance to meet. I began to understand the mindset of these people and, in doing so, I finally started to see *it*.

What is *it*? you ask. *It* is the people that most employees don't know due to lack of exposure, the individuals most employees feel they can't touch. I began to build relationships. I finally had the opportunity to utilize great minds in order to benefit my growth. I'm not saying I used people, but I am guilty of using their expert advice to aid in my growth. Great leaders are great listeners first! And even today I reflect on my journey and maybe my road isn't as long and hard as others, but my persistence to succeed is relentless and has aided me in going past the mark that many people would think of as an obstacle. Great leaders do not let time disorient them from their goals and outlook on things.

After graduating from the associate program, I was in a role that provided me with plenty of responsibility. There was always room for improvement, room to be taught more, and room to succeed. To my peers it seemed that I had achieved success, but I hadn't. I still had a hunger to achieve something that I have yet to define. And that hunger still motivates me to this day. That hunger motivates me to share my story with people and to give them the message: never become complacent.

CHAPTER X

I Built on Things I Already Possessed

The question is posed to me, "Derrick, what makes you a leader? Why do you feel you were chosen?" There are things that happened to me in my life that I can't explain and there are plenty that I can. Some were the result of natural tendencies, some the result of trying too hard to be a figure, an icon, someone I wanted to be rather than who I actually was. I created a false image about myself, the real Derrick, and my background, a persona that was greater than I actually was. There were times when I seemed angrier, bigger, and braver than I truly was, and the only person who suffered the consequences of those actions was me.

Through my college years I had good times, but I also had bad times. I had trials, bad situations, and I did things I should not have done. I still get frustrated over some of the things I have done in the past, but, by the grace of God, I've moved to a different stage of my life, and I'm comfortable that those things are forgiven.

What makes me a leader? Ever since my youth, I've had a natural tendency to lead. People followed me and I didn't know why at times; maybe they saw something in me that I didn't see in myself. Maybe God had a vision that covered the hurt I was going through in order for me to grow and to realize that who I am is who He wanted me to be. Not until my later years, and I'm referring to my late twenties, did I really start to cultivate the attributes in myself that I saw as leadership. Maybe it took people of power, or who I imagined had power, saying that I would be a great leader one day. Maybe that shook me a little, to realize that there was something to what people were saying. I didn't have to go beyond what was there in order to prove who I am and who God made me to be.

Now I'm coming into my own. At this stage of my life, I've embraced change in a corporation, which finally made me cultivate what I thought were my leadership abilities. I began to practice and correct things I needed to change about myself. I started taking notes on what people grasped as my strengths and I began to invest in them. I started training myself. I was learning, communicating, and speaking. It's funny how we will train ourselves not to be a success when God already has it in our plans for us to be a success. We will train ourselves not to be great communicators, not to be leaders, and not to be devoted to our goals. We train ourselves out of those things because we don't recognize what our natural abilities are. Instead, we try to create a persona, and end up trying to grasp things we can't hold on to. We allow those things to disturb our growth and they infringe on our natural attributes. We let ourselves go; we jump out of God's hands because we want to do it on our own.

Great leaders build on what they already possess. They mold things about themselves and become experts on their natural self. Until you know who you are, you can't benefit anyone else with your leadership skills. One of my mentors told me at one point in my life, "You have to be innovative enough to continue to create opportunity for yourself." And after he told me this, I asked myself, "What am I better than average at, and how have I increased or built upon those traits?" I found that, in order to be happy in this world, we have to be happy with ourselves. In other words, we have to be completely confident in our self progression; from that, we give testimony to someone else about facts rather than imagination.

I ask myself all the time, what do you want to be, Derrick? The answer is simple: I want to be who He made me to be. I want to be that helpmate, father, friend, that individual that helps someone out of his or her struggle. Ultimately, helping people enriches me; it builds my character, and it creates an energy around me that is attractive to those who share that same devotion to helping.

The more similar the ideas, the more hearts at peace and in prayer, the bigger the push will be for people to stop destroying each other. We will want to be who we are as opposed to putting on an image of who we want to be. And being who we are does not mean staying constant, but it means building upon those natural attributes God gave us. I hate that it took me twenty-some odd years to realize that, because now I'm starting to build on what God provided me instead of trying to create this false perception of myself.

Why do I think I have been chosen? I have seen all the people whom I resembled in character. I've seen people who talked as I talked, viewed things as I viewed things, and were as possessive of material things as I was. I saw all of these people, and those people failed in front of me. Those people didn't succeed at what they thought they would be a success at. And by seeing those people, God showed me you can be one of those people who you see falling before you, or you can choose to learn from them. Of course, I chose to learn and benefit from those examples because some of those people who crumbled before me had exalted themselves and, during high school and college, I, too, exalted myself. God brought me down until I couldn't go down any more; He told me that I needed to see these things that were happening to me. I needed to see these things around me, to stop riding my fake elevator to the sky and to look around me. Did I want to be like these people? Did I want people to view me like this? Did I want people to talk about me like they were talking about them? No. I didn't want that person to be me. I have been given opportunities that I can't explain to this very day. And I will not give a school, a book, or any other object the credit. I give all the credit to God.

Even after college, I did things that I look back on and realize, "Boy, that was stupid." But in having a relationship with God, I understand from Him that, until I use those things which He has given me to benefit His kingdom, I will use them to destroy myself. Those same things that glorify me, that exalt me in men's eyes, will destroy me.

Often things happen to us that we have no control over, but we can control how we use them. There are situations in our lives that we can't control, but we can control how we learn from them. God has instilled in us something that nobody else has; we have a special quality that God needs for His edification. But until we use it to benefit Him, it will destroy us.

What does it take? How much time do I have to devote? Who will be involved? Can I make it on my own? Can I offer up 50% of my mind and cover the gaps as I go? Oh, many want the position, but does your resume indicate that you are a qualified candidate? Have you been working long enough to have a validated work history on your resume? Leaders are not made by word of mouth. Leaders are not made by how many good references someone else gives them. Leaders are not made by how many material items they own. But leaders are made by the example they live and the witnesses they have gained through the fruits they bear. Good leaders make everyone feel they belong to the success of the body. And, when you have ownership of something, there is more meaning behind your accomplishment. Are we attentive to those around us? Each one of us has room to be a great leader, but do we adapt to change around us in order to build upon our potential? By powerfully communicating a vision that animates, motivates, and inspires followers, a great leader is able to transform his or her following.

CHAPTER XI

Start with 'I'

In order to do that, leaders start with the 'I's first and then move forward. What are the 'I's? Basically, the 'I's are a descriptive composition of self. We have to be intuitive, interactive, innovative, and integrated in order to become efficient in leading. This sounds complicated to apply, but it's really a simple gesture. Too many times we point the finger at someone or something that prevents us from accomplishing what we set out to accomplish. We don't investigate ourselves enough to understand why it is that we are failing at becoming what or who we want to be. Great leaders have to become intuitive, interactive, innovative, and integrated in order to lead effectively. Allow me to expound upon "starting with 'I'."

To be intuitive means to possess or to demonstrate intuition, to become instinctive. Great leaders have minds that become crowded with information. How can one possibly store everything that one hears, sees, and learns one's whole life? One would think there is a point of overload. Where is the reserve that we go to when we get to this point? How do leaders keep their composure when entering the red area of memory overload? The answer is simple: not only do they rely on others, but most importantly they rely on their intuitive thought process. No longer do they pull stored information, but they exhibit a learned behavior that allows them to react mentally without appearing to think about it. And some may ask the question, well, wouldn't I be guessing if I used this logic? The answer is no. You have information stored in your subconscious that allows you to create and extract from others what may be needed at the time.

How valuable is an intuitive leader to most corporations today? I say their value is priceless! Who wouldn't want a visionary problem-solver, someone who can forecast the dangers that may be lurking? Leaders have to rely on their intuition every day. It's not possible to keep every single piece of information you have received in your head over the years. But you can act on your intuition and save yourself from trouble in a lot of instances. Great military leaders don't become great by waiting to give a decision under extreme circumstances. Many times it's their intuitive thinking that saved the lives of others. Many consider this a gift, but, from my experience, I believe we all possess an intuitive thought process. How it is activated becomes the Achilles heel to many.

This question deserves attention: how is our intuition activated? To my knowledge we have to be interactive with someone or something in order to start this process. Being interactive requires working together so the total effect is greater than the individual efforts of those involved. Leaders interact with others on a continuous basis. It necessary in order to lead.

Growing up, my uncle had to interact with me and my cousins when we helped him work on houses and do different odd jobs. If he hadn't, most of the time my cousins and I would have wandered off, doing things our own way. So he constantly had to instruct us, demonstrate and show us what he wanted done, and make sure we carried out his instructions. This allowed him to focus on his vision, the final product, and, because there was interaction, the project would be completed to his satisfaction. And the more he interacted with me, the more I learned from him. Before my uncle trained me, I had no knowledge of how to build an addition or to shingle a house. But, due to his training, I developed those skills over time. In effect, I assumed his leadership characteristics because I became efficient enough at following his instructions that I no longer required constant interaction. There was more time for him to work alongside me instead of teaching me.

There is a lesson to be learned here. Great leaders should operate in a way that minimizes their distractions. You lead by training, directly or indirectly. In your training, you expect those receiving your instructions to acquire procedural skills. What does this do? It shows your followers that you are not beyond relationship-building. Interaction allows relationships to form and creates an understanding between parties. We help others build confidence by giving them an opportunity to take ownership of a task. This simple process gives leaders room to become innovative in their efforts to increase performance.

An innovative leader is one that always stays ahead of the current. His ideas are fresh, original, and inspire change from the normal way of doing things. This brings to mind a young, ambitious individual who had the innovative idea to separate red blood cells from plasma, freezing the two. This innovative discovery would save the lives of millions by allowing blood to be preserved and reconstituted for later use. You may have heard of the institution where he served as a director and led an effort to collect and bank blood on a large scale, the American Red Cross. This gentleman, Charles Drew, revolutionized the medical profession and received the Spingarn Medal in 1944 for his innovative thoughts.

I could go on for days about individuals who, because of their innovative ideas, changed the lives of millions in some capacity. Where is the innovation in our day-to-day thoughts? Is there any at all? Do we push ourselves out of our old thought processes? We buy new cars and clothes because our previous ones have gotten old. They get old to us because we change. The same concept applies to our thinking: if we don't change as time progresses, we become stuck in our thought processes.

Leaders must become integrated into time. We ask ourselves how we can become integrated into something that always changes. When leaders become integrated with their environments, they produce solutions, which allow organizations to quickly leverage and determine availability of resources, thereby improving asset utilization (their people), and enhancing service quality (the customer). Leaders promote visibility and facilitate the application of real-time solutions. Simply put, we always have to be on our toes, because people want answers, right now! We need help, we need organization, and we need to become integrated with our peers. Leaders must utilize individuals that are available to them and exploit their strengths.

This sounds harsh, but it's really not; it's a concept many successful leaders use. How we mold and empower others determines our dependency upon them as a leader. We must see success around every corner.

CHAPTER XII

My Measure of Success

Trying to appease people causes us to limit our creative process. What makes a success a success, a victory a victory? It's not winning at all cost, but what we measure from it. Our happiness defines a success, what we conclude from our story, and what we conclude from the journey we have traveled. Are we satisfied with where we are? Is there pleasure in our hearts with who we are? Our measure of success is normally our own happiness. Winning, victory, these things are within. If we leave our success up to other individuals, a lot of times we will fail. We focus on money more often than we make ourselves students of the process to obtain money. Many people want millions of dollars. This would make many happy. But the reality that many refuse to recognize is that the money itself won't make us happy, but the things that you do with the money may provide some measure of contentment.

I asked many people, if I presented them with a dollar bill or a sheet of paper and pen, which they would choose. Overwhelmingly many chose the dollar bill, which proves my point that money is a perceived value of wealth. This is not a new-found discovery. Many have made this claim long before my time, I'm just piggy-backing off it. What will a dollar bill buy you these days? A cold soda? Bag of chips? Candy bar, or maybe a hot dog? All of these items are temporary and will surely perish after use. So where is the sustainability in choosing the dollar bill?

At this stage in my life, I would undoubtedly choose the sheet of paper. A sheet of paper can serve as a medium to write a letter to a loved one that will be cherished. It can serve as a medium to start a book that may inspire and change the lives of millions. It can illustrate a drawing of an invention that could save someone's life. By now you get my point of perceived value. We have to apply the same creative thinking to our lives; we have to perceive greatness in everything we do.

How do we create opportunities for ourselves? Many of us wait. We want someone else or something else to give us success. Our consciousness needs stroking. Do we have a better chance of feeling good about ourselves by our own assessment of our worth, or by someone else giving us a compliment? We will always feel better about ourselves through our own self-validation than we ever will through someone else's opinion. We have the opportunity to wake up every day and be thankful for something. We have the opportunity to tell ourselves for the rest of our lives that we WILL be victorious today.

Parents instill in their children the beliefs that they are going to be great, smart, and successful. We should develop the minds of our youngest generation. Once you internalize success, you will become a success. If you have control over yourself, then you will control your destiny and arrive at a point where you want to be. The keys to controlling your future are in your hands. You need to tell yourself what you are going to be. Quit relying on your surroundings to define who you are.

There are many people who grew up in poverty, but did not let poverty define their future. They were hungry for something more than just perishable items. Their situation presented them with the task not to live in poverty for the rest of their lives. Therefore, they set in motion the process to becoming mentally fit. They started to feed their mental capacity with things they could internalize, then externally act on.

When we need something from someone else, we become subject to them. But we need not live like we are controlled robots that someone else can turn on and off. The greatest CEOs never believe that people are working for them because of their own attributes. I would bet that what they are paying folks has a lot to do with it. But there are some people, who may not make the most in the company, who may not even be in the upper level of salary, whose value to the company is immeasurable. Some people are fooled into believing they have authority over us, yet it may be a simple control method that we have over them. Now, a lot of people will have problems with this. There are a lot of people who are empowering themselves with tools that are being financed by other entities. There are people who walk into work every day with the mindset of, "This is my building. I own my success!"

If, in fact, we believe that our strongest chess piece is our mind, why do we continue to feed the natural perishable items of this world? There is so much free knowledge in this world that we can be practically anything we want to be from a few internet searches. America the beautiful, the land where one can find hope, follow dreams; a land where education is simple to access, but also where children and adults are uneducated. Many students leave high school because they feel it's useless. School is not for them. Foreigners come to this land to gain access to resources because they are so plentiful. Foreigners come to this land, set up shop, own businesses, run companies, and we ask ourselves, "How can someone come from another country and be successful when I've lived here all my life and have nothing?" It's simple. They internalized what they could do with these assets and externally acted on them. So how can we be mad at someone who comes to the land of opportunity and capitalizes on the things it has to offer? What are we going to do? Will we continue to make excuses, complain about the assets that we refuse to use?

I stopped complaining and set in motion the process of utilizing these assets. How did I start utilizing these assets? There was a cleansing of my mind and soul, a renewing of a faith that lives deep within me and has brought forth fruit. There was an intervention of the Most High, which slowed my aggressive ways. My outward sign is no longer that of a raging bull ready to protect his territory, but one with a humble nature, an individual who understands that coexistence is a part of life, and realizes that everyone is not out to attack me. I became an individual who no longer felt the need to compete or be better, Derrick Barksdale, father, husband, student. I learned how to be a leader by trial. Yes, there were classes, but the homework for those classes was my life, the answer to the questions was my life. As one can see through this book, my life has been homework, a big research project to understand what it takes to be a leader in my eyes. I had to develop a harmony about myself that invited others to share in that harmony. I had to become nurturing to my home so that my home felt secure. I had to become an individual who stood as an example to a young man who shares my name. I had to become a statue to my wife who expects me to lead. And, by leading, I had to be focused, strong in my ways, spiritually clean, not blinded, but motivated to know about His existence. I took back my life, the parts that other people controlled. Now I have my own empire, now I have a puzzle that I hold all of the pieces to. I no longer get frustrated by how individuals view me or talk about me, because they have no control over my ultimate reward. Yet, some look with disbelief and still have the mindset that maybe I'm not good enough. And that's okay; we have to accept the fact that people will have opinions about us. But we have to be strong enough to discern that when we turn our fate over to another individual we become controlled by that same individual. We become subject to that person. Digest what is good, stay focused and be creative. You are rich in this world if you just believe! "His divine power has given us everything we need for life and godliness through our knowledge of Him who called us" (2 Peter 1:3, NIV). Follow your process; document it step by step. Take baby steps every day, and every day you can be assured that you are stepping closer to your ultimate goals. I have become closer to my ultimate goal by sharing my life with you, because now I've developed a network with people who share in my process. You can get out of your situation if it is not what you want it to be. Think your way out of it. Stop worrying about what you don't have. Instead, internalize the realization that you have everything you need in this world, and then you will find yourself giving away things because you have gained too much to handle. Allow determination to line your internal thinking.

CHAPTER XIII

My Final Steps to Victory

Determination, fixed intention, and firmness of purpose: do we align with these adjectives when acting on our goals of becoming successful leaders? See the end result, and allow your mind to take you there. Achieving the end result requires us to focus in on exactly what we are trying to achieve, and then create the steps to get there. These steps to victory include: thinking the part, speaking the part, moving, creating powerful associations, being consistent, and keeping a fruitful work ethic.

1. Think the part!

We have to believe we have power and authority.

Those who believe are moved towards those things conceived in their minds. Jesus, one of the greatest leaders to walk this earth once stated, "If thou canst believe, all things are possible to him that believeth" (Mark 9:23, KJV). People develop confidence in their learning because they believe in what is being taught. Believe in success, and you will find yourself consuming more than you could ever imagine. A repetitive thought has to be acted upon; it's a law of nature. The more something is told, taught, or recited to you by yourself, the media, or some other being, the more your mind begins to internalize it. And once your mind has internalized the thought, it begins to control your actions.

Wake up every day and start telling yourself that you are going to be a successful leader. I promise you things in your life are going to start moving in that direction. When I first entertained the thought of grad school, I kept telling myself, "You are crazy. It will never happen. You're just the average student. Don't do it." But if I did go to grad school, I thought about the opportunities that would come my way. So I began to think as if I already had obtained the degree. I started taking baby steps towards getting into business school and really didn't know why. Finally, I was accepted, went on to graduate, and was the first in my immediate family to achieve an advanced degree. Think the part!

2. Speak the part!

Powerful and authoritative people speak with certainty about their selected subjects. The image you paint of yourself involves more than just the visual; the sound also helps shape the subject. How persuasive are you if what you're saying does not sound like you are confident in the content? Many great leaders of today are some of the most prolific speakers of our time. They gain interest and support by communicating to people in a way that grabs hold of their attention. People speak with power and authority because they believe in what they are saying.

Great leaders speak the part because their content is well-prepared and well-planned. Their final product comes out of their mouths as it does because careful planning went into shaping it. Speaking the part does not mean just saying something loud and forcefully, but elegantly displaying an arrangement of words that not only sounds enticing, but comes to life in people's minds. The more we as leaders entertain the mind, the more people will show up for the concert. Speak the part!

3. Move

Quit standing still in your growth. Your life is a description of who you really are.You have to grow, and growing means studying, praying, being obedient, and moving towards that higher place in your life that brings you abundance. This is not the same place for many people, and that's okay. Abundance, to many, does not equate to millions of dollars; it may just be a way of life. But, in order to achieve abundance, no matter what it equates to, you have to move towards it. Many people lose what God has provided them because they refuse to move in a direction to maintain it.

How many times have you told yourself what you need to do, but it remained just that, an order to yourself? You will never complete the race that you're running if you don't take the first step towards the finish line. No race is ever won by an individual standing still. Your growth towards becoming a successful leader has to do with how much momentum you put behind your goals.

If you had a ball and were standing on top of a hill, all you would need to do is give that ball a slight tap and it would go barreling down the hill. Think of your growth in the same manner. With the right angle and slope of the hill, one little step can turn into a mountain of success. The summer before my 9th grade year, I knew that, in order to compete with the other kids physically, I had to do more than the average. I needed to be faster and stronger than I was, so I began to lift weights and run when I knew nobody was making me do it. I began to move towards the goals I wanted to achieve, and I didn't wait for the first day of practice to do so. Too often we live a life of waiting for someone else to direct us instead of giving ourselves tailored directions. And while we are waiting for someone else to deliver our directions, we end up standing still. Today is the day we stop standing still in our growth, and move!

4. Create powerful associations.

You are who you are, not on your own account or ability, but by your association with the Most High. How can you become a successful leader? Study those who are already there. Great leaders have mentors, people they talk to, family, etc. In some form or fashion, the people you associate with will change your social structure and attitudes towards success. If you want to learn how to be a brick mason, what do you do? You guessed it: you go talk to and work with a brick mason to learn his craft. The same principle applies to leadership: if you want to be a powerful leader, you learn from a powerful leader. Too often we put ourselves around the "I can't" people, and we start believing in the same manner. You have heard the old saying "misery loves company"; well, it's true in a lot of cases.

We have created a social norm of associating ourselves with people who are just like us, instead of with people who we aspire to be like. I found mentors throughout my life and became their student because I saw something in them that I needed. Now, does this mean go out and get all new friends and family members? I think not. But you do have to start seeking individuals who are at or above the position you are trying to achieve in life. I use the word "powerful" because these associations need to mean something to you. What good are they if the information being received is going in one ear and out the other? The associations need to be with people who are living what you are dreaming. And by creating these powerful associations, you start gaining the characteristics by becoming the prized pupil of your associations.

5. Be consistent and maintain clarity.

You have to listen in order to be led so that you become an influential leader. When we are faithful to what God has ordained for us to do, we become consistent at doing it. You are faithful at keeping your house and car, so you maintain a job to do so. Even when you don't want to go to work, you remain consistent for fear of losing what you have; therefore, you follow a weekly routine that sustains your way of living. Great leaders are consistent and maintain clarity in seeking their goals.

If you continue to keep, maintain, and entertain clutter around you, then you will inherit a cluttered mind. If things around you are not in order, then it will be hard to know where to go to get what you need when you need it. Let me apply that to your daily lives. If you keep clutter all over your home, there is going to come a time when you will need that one item, but, because you refused to maintain clarity in your home, it is difficult to find it. Great leaders are consistent and clear on their direction, for if they are confusing, no one would follow them. Confusion leads to inconsistency, which leads to a fumbling of thoughts and direction.

Leaders are clear in their direction. They eliminate confusion and frustration from situations. They recognize there are situations they have to face, and use them for fuel. They exert discipline in their situation, which directs and guides their subconscious mindset. They tailor their environments to eliminate distractions, and keep those following focused on their goals. Be consistent and maintain clarity in your strides to become a leader.

6. Keep a fruitful work ethic.

Let every action towards your success as a leader becomes a fruitful one. Simply put, make sure your efforts bring forth positive things. Do you work to maintain your way of living, or to increase your value? Simple question but hard to digest. Many Americans, no matter the income, work just to maintain their way of living. There is no dramatic increase in savings, stocks, etc., but just enough money is coming in to pay the bills. Surely this is not the life we want for ourselves as valued leaders. Your work ethic should bring you a fruitful return. Allow your work ethic to grow in you so that your final product yields abundant returns.

How would a farmer feel if he spent months preparing for a fruitful season, and nothing ever grew? Destroyed, he would feel that all of his hard work was in vain. Do you feel that way about your life right now? If so, today is the day to start planning for a successful crop. If not, keep doing what you are doing, and you may never produce abundance. Great leaders maintain a work ethic that is fruitful in order that they increase. Your margin of increase depends on how well you prepare for it.

You must realize that you are your number one supporter. Continue to take steps towards becoming great. Quit hiring actors to play the part and become the part yourself.

My grandmother was never given to a flashy lifestyle. I'm talking about a woman who lived her whole life focused on what she has presented to this world as her most precious gift, her family. Holiday after holiday, we assembled together as a family, sharing in each other's joys, talking about each other's past, and motivating each other towards the future. True leaders are proud of their accomplishments, and have solid products to show for their hard work. Whether it is family, goals, or quality of life, devote your whole life to making it better so that you can appreciate the product you created. I learned from my grandmother what it takes to become a true leader. Many men of this world characterize women as a gender not fit to lead in a kingdom, even though they have no authority to delegate positions in it. This prestigious position my grandmother holds was not appointed by man, but by a spiritual authority, rushing through to reward her for her noble works.

Many do not recognize leaders that are in their presence. The sorghum press, that solid, erect, unmovable machine, has maintained its presence since way before my existence. No matter what the elements, its legacy will remain. I played around that press all my life, stood on it, and sometimes tried to move it to no avail, not realizing what it was, what it had been through, and the symbol it had become. Things come to life around us to make us who we are. My Sorghum Press has come to life; now well into my adult years, I see its meaning, its position, and everything it has taught me over the years without completely understanding what it was. Now I understand: it is a symbol of the struggling soldier who has made it through turbulent times, and now victory is the word that describes my grandmother's journey. Love what you are and become nothing less than who He made you to be. If you think it, you can achieve it; if you believe it can happen, then it already has happened. Realize that the greatness in you has been there all of your life; you just have to see and understand what makes it great, then appreciate just that about it.

Today is the day you tell yourself, "I will think and speak the part to move myself in a direction that creates powerful associations, in order that I may be consistent and clear in my quest, while maintaining a fruitful work ethic."

Tribute to my Son

The sun shining brightly, my heart racing, smiling, knowing something I've waited for since my young adult years has arrived. What a joy to experience such a gift and what a pain to remember a past that I've tried so hard to escape. My son, my shining light, my relief from the pain I have suffered for so long, is now concrete. To hold him in my arms is like no other feeling I can imagine. How I will protect him, prepare him, and love him runs through my head a million times. But knowing that I must love him keeps my thoughts concentrated on just that.

With odds stacked against me, my joy for having him overshadows the pain I've experienced for so long being without what I have now become. Father, Daddy, Dad, Old Man— I would give everything in this world just to be able to say those words to my father. Reaching constantly for something I cannot touch has only made me stronger. The strength I possess will be passed on, but multiplied by a thousand, to my son, Derrick Tyrone Barksdale II. Every day I wake up, I thank the Lord for this precious gift, and for giving me the opportunity to correct what has troubled my past.

The crying, the sleepless nights have all been erased by the blessings of changing a diaper, and feeding my son a bottle. I get on my knees and pray constantly that nothing will ever happen to interrupt the peaceful harmony called family, which I have created.

Derrick II deserves more than just a kiss on the cheek. He deserves an opportunity, and, with a strong woman to nurture our foundation, I will be that rock, that pillar, that God-fearing man. I will be a good husband to his mother, his best friend, and the father that he needs. That is how much my son means to me. He is an opportunity for me to be great. God has His hands on my future, and knowing that lets me know my son will be great, because he is a blessing from above.